Buddhism
for AS students

by Wendy Dossett
Series Editor: Roger J Owen

Teachers' Handbook

Buddhism

Acknowledgements

The author and publishers would like to thank the following for permission to reproduce copyright material in this book:

Buddhism, edited by Peter Harvey, 2001, Continuum International Publishing Company: p. 2, 20, 41; *The Foundations of Buddhism* by Rupert Gethin, 1998, reprinted by permission of Oxford University Press: p. 7, 26, 33; *Buddhism* by Denise Cush, 1993, reproduced by permission of Hodder and Stoughton Educational. Copyright 1993 Denise Cush p.12, 16; Extract from *The Buddhist Handbook* by John Snelling, 1998, published by Rider. Used by permission of the Random House Group Limited: p. 24; *Buddhism – A Very Short Introduction* by Damien Keown, 1996, reprinted by permission of Oxford University Press: p. 28, 37.

Every effort has been made to contact copyright holders of material reproduced in this publication. Any omission will be rectified in subsequent printings if notice is given to the publisher. While the information in this publication is believed to be true and accurate at the date of going to press, neither the author nor the publisher can accept any legal responsibility for any errors or omissions that may be made.

The author would like to thank Rhian Davies of King Henry VIII School, Abergavenny, for her advice in the preparation of this handbook.

Roger J Owen, Series Editor

Roger J Owen was Head of RE in a variety of schools for thirty years, as well as being a Head of Faculty, advisory teacher for primary and secondary RE, Section 23 Inspector and 'O' Level and GCSE Chief Examiner. Author of seventeen educational titles, he is currently an education consultant and WJEC Religious Studies AS and A2 Chair of Examiners.

Published by UWIC Press
UWIC, Cyncoed Road,
Cardiff CF23 6XD
cgrove@uwic.ac.uk
029 2041 6515

ISBN 1-902724-59-3

Design by *the info group*
Printed by *Pink Panther*

Commissioned with the financial assistance of Awdurdod Cymwysterau, Cwricwlwm ac Asesu Cymru / the Qualifications, Curriculum and Assessment Authority for Wales (ACCAC).

Buddhism
for AS students

by Wendy Dossett
Series Editor: Roger J Owen

Teachers' Handbook

Contents

Introduction

This handbook is designed to be used alongside the student textbook on Buddhism, also published by UWIC Press. The introduction to the student book states that it should not be seen as the sole textbook for the course, since advanced study requires the skills of wide reading, and the analysis of scholarly views on different issues. The same must said of the teachers' book. Whilst the two together provide ideas for the study of Buddhism at AS level, they do not obviate the need for further research and lesson preparation on the part of the teacher, and the study of additional texts, internet research and educational visits to Buddhist centres, museum exhibitions and so on, on the part of the student.

Part One of the teachers' book is designed to be used alongside the student textbook on a chapter-by-chapter basis, largely to facilitate differentiation. Further support material provides help with some of the tasks set in the student book. However, these tasks, and the others which appear in the teachers' book, should be seen as suggestions only. In particular the sections headed 'Key features of this discussion might include . . . ' should be seen as stimuli only. Discussions, when they go well, are dynamic and wide-ranging, and both teachers and students will doubtless wish to respond to questions with different observations from those set out here. This is to be welcomed and encouraged.

Each chapter of Part One contains questions that can be used either as written tasks, or as questions for a quiz, or for revision purposes. These may provide opportunities for the learning enhancement of lower-ability students, many of whom are taking up the opportunity to study Religious Studies at AS level. Most of these questions require merely single words or phrases to answer them. Later questions in each section become more challenging, thus allowing some differentiation.

A photocopiable self-assessment form is provided and can be adapted for use in each chapter. It will enable students to reflect on the strengths and weaknesses of their own learning, and to summarise important pieces of information for revision purposes. Each chapter also provides suggestions for further sources of information amongst the books most likely to be on the shelves of those teaching Buddhism at AS, and highlights useful websites.

In addition, teachers are encouraged to augment the information and ideas here by providing students with opportunities for demonstrating cross-curricular skills and utilising interactive methodologies. Art, drama, music and creative writing can be effective means of reinforcing factual knowledge, testing understanding and stimulating critical appreciation.

For example, groups of students could create a collage expressing one of the Three Marks of Existence or re-enact in mime the Four Sights. They could individually write a poem or produce an abstract piece of art to convey their feelings after a visit to a Buddhist temple or shrine room. Student-led seminars on specific topics (such as unique features of different schools of Buddhism) and peer marking, using the WJEC Religious Studies AS level descriptors, might also be incorporated into the teaching programme.

Part Two contains some specimen answers of varying qualities, and notes on how these answers would be marked.

WJEC Materials

Teachers will also wish to use the WJEC's own Religious Studies publications, including:
Specification; Teacher's Guide; Glossary of Key Terms; Specimen Questions and Mark Schemes;
Examiners' Reports.

These publications offer extensive guidance on course content, recommended books, approaches to examinations (including the understanding of 'trigger words' in examination questions) and the assessment objective level descriptors. Naturally these are essential tools for anyone teaching Religious Studies at AS level.

Key Skills in Religious Studies

The WJEC Specification (Religious Studies 550, 2003) includes a detailed analysis of the Key Skills which are to be developed and assessed through the AS course (see WJEC Specification, Chapter 3, and Appendix 1, 2 and 3). The key skills are defined as:

- Communication **(KS/C)**
- Information technology **(KS/IT)**
- Problem solving **(KS/PS)**

- Working with others **(KS/WO)**
- Improving own learning and performance **(KS/ILP)**

The student textbook and this teachers' handbook provide ample opportunities to develop and assess these skills through a range of student tasks. Each of the student tasks is coded using the above codes, to indicate which Key Skills opportunities are being offered in a particular task.

Spiritual, moral, ethical and cultural issues

The WJEC AS Specification for Religious Studies highlights the aspects of the specification that may contribute to the spiritual and moral development of students.

What appears below is an adaptation of the specification paragraphs appropriate to the study of Buddhism at AS. Most of the bullet points are covered in each of the students'/ teachers' books, and all are addressed during the study of Buddhism at AS level.

1.6.5 The various modules provide ample scope for studies which might contribute to candidates **spiritual devolvement**. All modules directly address subject matter which is concerned with:
- The quest for meaning in life, truth and ultimate values;
- Awareness of aspects of human life other than the physical and material;
- Human experiences of transcendence or wonder and mystery;
- The exploration of religious beliefs; and provide a stimulus for candidates to:
- Explore their own beliefs, creative abilities, insights, self-identity, and self-worth;
- Recognise and value the world and others.

1.6.6 In like manner, the modules offer extensive scope for contributing to an understanding of **moral, ethical, social and cultural issues**. All the world religions modules provide opportunities to
- Study relationships between religion and culture;
- Consider moral values and attitudes of individuals, faith communities or contemporary society;
- Develop skill in reasoning on matters concerning values, attitudes and actions;
- Develop the ability to make responsible judgements on significant moral teaching and issues.

Part One: Support material for each chapter

Section 1: The Life of the Buddha

Chapter 1: India at the Time of the Buddha

When using this chapter in the classroom it is important to remember that it is an account of the background to the Buddha's life and teachings. You should ensure that students do not confuse the traditions of Brahmanism with the teachings of the Buddha. In fact there are good reasons for giving a brief outline of the life of the Buddha and his teachings before focussing on the contents of this chapter, in order to make sure the students are clear about the difference between the Indian background to Buddhism, and Buddhism itself. This approach will help students to make sense of some of the recommended reading.

Questions for revision

1. What is the Sanskrit word for soul?
2. What does tat tvam asi mean?
3. What does the phrase 'atman is Brahman' mean?
4. What is transmigration?
5. What is karma?
6. What is moksha?
7. What is dharma?
8. Explain the varna system.
9. Explain ritual purity.
10. Why did sramanas break their ties with family and community?

Answers can be found on page 47.

Further resources for the study of India at the time of the Buddha

Cush, Denise	Buddhism	5-11
Harvey, Peter	Buddhism	4-5
Harvey, Peter	An Introduction to Buddhism: Teaching, History and Practices	9-14
Skilton, Andrew	A Concise History of Buddhism	3-18
Snelling, John	The Buddhist Handbook	3-19
Gethin, Rupert	The Foundations of Buddhism	7-13

Reading

From *Buddhism*, edited by Peter Harvey, Continuum, 2001 p5

'[The Buddha] lived his life in a religious context in which an early form of Hinduism generally known as 'Brahmanism' or 'Vedic religion' was of considerable influence. The teachings of [the Buddha] shared certain basic ideas with Brahmanism, for example karma and rebirth, the goal of liberation from this, the existence of gods, yogic practices, and the valuing of spiritual insight. Nevertheless, his ideas on these were different from that of the Brahmin priests and he clearly differed from Brahmanism in that he did not accept certain key features of their world-view. He did not accept their scriptures as at all authoritative and also did not accept: the efficacy of sacrifices to the gods and the killing of animals involved in this; the idea of a divinely ordained social system of four varnas, which became the basis for the later system of many castes; and the idea that a person contains a permanent, fixed Self. Even where he shared ideas such as karma and rebirth, he did not accept these from the existing culture. For one thing, they were relatively new ideas, and were challenged by some of the renuncian... communities that rejected Brahmanism and which in some ways resembled Greek philosophical movements. Amongst these were the Jains and the Buddhists themselves, both of which accepted some form of karma and rebirth doctrine; but the materialists rejected karma and rebirth, the sceptics were agnostic on them and the Ajivakas were fatalists who believed that one's rebirth was determined by a blind impersonal fate, not one's freely chosen karma (action). For another thing, [the Buddha] felt that his meditative experiences gave him direct evidence of past lives, in the form of memories, and of the way in which the quality of a person's karma affected his or her future rebirth. Thus it would be wrong to see Buddhism as 'arising from Hinduism' both because of what has been said already, and because what we now call Hinduism is a culmination of various changes arising from Brahmanism drawing on a variety of popular cults. Moreover, Hinduism was in part influenced by ideas drawn from Buddhism, which was a rival religion in India.'

Questions
1) What were the views of: a) the Ajivakas; b) the Brahmans?
2) What features of Brahmanism did the Buddha reject?
3) What features of Brahmanism did the Buddha accept?
4) What reasons does Peter Harvey give for saying that it would be wrong to see Buddhism as arising from Hinduism?

Further information for tasks set in students' book

KS/C KS/IT KS/WO KS/ILP

How does this definition of the soul compare to ideas to be found in other religions?

Resources for this discussion

Quotation from Chambers Dictionary of Beliefs and Religions, Edinburgh 1992
A generic definition of the soul:
'Soul: the seat of the personality; the life-force which animates human beings, a synonym for self or mind. The concept derives from Plato for whom it was a metaphysical entity, ultimately incorruptible and eternal. In religious thought the soul is often regarded as the divine or immortal element imprisoned in the human body. At death the soul is liberated from the body and continues to exist in disembodied form or is reincarnated in a new body.'

The following website might be helpful:
www.hinduwebsite.com/hinduism/atma.htm

Key features of this discussion might include:
* Differences between eschatological teachings and transmigrational teaching;
* Relationship between soul and body, soul and personality or personhood.

KS/C KS/IT KS/WO KS/ILP

Is it reasonable to believe in reincarnation? If so, why, if not, why not?

Resources for this discussion

An exploration of the following websites will be fruitful:
www.comparativereligion.com/reincarnation

This is a Christian site dedicated to the de-bunking of Hindu and Buddhist ideas. It has some very interesting investigations of karma and reincarnation which are presented as if 'objective'. However, the information provided here is good quality, so long as it is read with an awareness of the aim of the writer. There are many references to the work of Ian Stevenson, who has researched the accounts of children's past lives, one of the most quoted pieces of 'evidence' for reincarnation. Inevitably the writer concludes that there is no acceptable evidence for reincarnation (and even goes so far as to explain why the apparent references to reincarnation in the Bible are misinterpreted as such).

Students might compare the essays in this website with the accounts of karma and reincarnation on the following Hindu websites.
www.karamsad.com/reincarnation.htm
www.karamsad.com/karma.htm
www.hinduwebsite.com/conceptofkarma.htm

Key feature of this discussion might include:
- The value of 'scientific proof' (hypnosis, childhood accounts of past lives, the 'testing' performed to discover reincarnated teachers in the Tibetan tradition);
- Whether the doctrine of reincarnation makes sense of the differences between us;
- Whether the idea of past and future lives is any more/less reasonable than the idea of an afterlife heaven/hell;
- Whether there are any moral or philosophical objections to belief in reincarnation – is it deterministic?
- Whether it makes any sense to believe in an immortal soul, the essence of the person, which transmigrates.

Discussion should go beyond the simplistic notion that if you do bad things you come back as a slug, or student speculation about what they might like to come back as next time!

Seminar topic p. 3   KS/C KS/WO KS/ILP

Many religions ask their followers to renounce things for spiritual reasons (e.g. fasting during Ramadan, or giving up something during Lent). Why do you think this is?

Key features of this discussion might include:
- The identification with those who are poor, hungry, or going without in other ways;
- The attainment of a sense of community with others who are engaged in the same practice;
- The fulfilment of a commandment believed to have a divine source;
- The development of discipline as a virtue;
- The making of a sacrifice in imitation of a religious figure (e.g. Jesus);
- In some religions there might be a health aspect – a purified body helps meditation;
- The belief that the needs and desires of the body must be overcome for spiritual development or in order to attain spiritual release.

Research task p. 3   KS/C KS/IT KS/WO KS/PS KS/ILP

Using the Internet and other sources, discover examples of the austerities of modern day sadhus. The festival of the Kumbh Mela in 2001 saw many thousands of sadhus perform their austerities in the same place. Try to explain their intentions.

Additional resources for this task
The following websites will be helpful:
www.kumbhallabad.com   www.kumbhmela.com
www.channel4.com/kumbhmela/kumbharama.html

For a more detailed and beautifully illustrated study of sadhus, see Dolf Hartsuiker's Sadhus, Holy Men of India, Thames and Hudson, London, 1993. Key features might include:
1) The control of the body's needs and desires;
2) The overcoming of aversion;
3) The aim of moksha;
4) The emphasis on mental renunciation over physical mortification.

Explain the importance of the belief in atman to ancient Indians at the time of the Buddha.

Key features of this answer might include:
- Reference to some of the reading mentioned above;
- Atman as the eternal essence of a person which transmigrates and according to some the Upanishadic teachings is identical with Brahman;
- Related ideas about karma, reincarnation and moksha;
- An awareness of the different schools of thought around at the time of the Buddha, e.g. the Ajivakas, the Jains and the Sceptics, who all had slightly different ideas about the relationship between atman and karma;
- Recognition that in some traditions, the atman attains release as a result of extreme ascetic practices;
- An awareness that the Buddha was to criticise the notion of atman.

Sometimes Buddhism is described as an 'experiential religion', which means in part that it is only fully understood by those that practise it. Is this a problem for AS level study? If it is, what can we do to overcome this problem?

Opportunities for Synoptic Element preparation

It would be advisable for students to make notes in preparation for the A2 Synoptic Assessment in areas which include:

- **Religious Authority**
  Authority of the Vedas and the Brahmins rejected by the Buddha.
- **Religious Experience**
  Experience of liberation of those following extreme ascetic paths, which was later to impress the Buddha and to be his aim for the six years immediately prior to his enlightenment.
- **Life, Death and Life After Death**
  The Indian notions of atman, karma and transmigration, which the Buddha was later to reject or modify.

Note to teachers
The word Brahman has two main meanings. When it means priest it is sometimes anglicised to Brahmin. Brahmanism is the priestly, ritual-orientated religion of the Buddha's time. When the term Brahman is used in this discussion it should not be confused with the term for Ultimate Reality, which is also Brahman.

Chapter 2: Key Events in the Life of the Buddha

An important feature of work with this chapter is that students go beyond simply learning the traditional stories. AS questions are likely to ask for explanation, which requires students to do more than merely recount events. Often questions will be about the meaning of the story to Buddhists, about the importance of historicity, or they might be trying to elicit personal evaluative responses to aspects of the Buddha's life. This may appear to be an 'easy' topic area on the specification, but it is a treacherous one for those students who do not demonstrate the higher order skills.

Questions for revision

These questions are about key events in the life of the Buddha.
11. What does Shakyamuni mean?
12. Name the Buddha's parents.
13. What did Asita prophecy?
14. What were the Four Sights?
15. Why did Siddhartha leave the palace?
16. What did Siddhartha see during the first watch of the night under the Bodhi tree?
17. Why is Nirvana difficult to define?
18. What is Mahaparinirvana?
19. Explain the Buddha's last words.
20. Explain why the Buddha's death is an inspiration to Buddhists.

Answers can be found on pages 47-48.

Further resources for the study of the Life of the Buddha

Cush, Denise	Buddhism	6-24
Keown, Damien	Buddhism: A Very Short Introduction	14-28
Harvey, Peter	An Introduction to Buddhism: Teaching, History and Practices	14-29
Skilton, Andrew	A Concise History of Buddhism	19-24
Snelling, John	The Buddhist Handbook	20-40
Gethin, Rupert	The Foundations of Buddhism	7-27

From *The Foundations of Buddhism* by Rupert Gethin, OUP, 1998 p16

'Of course, as the Buddhist tradition tells it, the story of the life of the Buddha is not history nor meant to be. The whole story takes on a mythic and legendary character. A wealth of detail is brought in capable of being read metaphorically, allegorically, typologically, and symbolically. Much of this detail is to modern sensibilities of a decidedly 'miraculous' and 'supernatural' kind. The story of the Buddha's life becomes not an account of the particular and individual circumstances of a man who, some 2,500 years ago left home to become a wandering ascetic, but something universal, an archetype; it is the story of all those who have become Buddhas in the past and all who will become Buddhas in the future, and in a sense, of all who follow the Buddhist path. It is the story of the Buddhist path, a story which shows the way to a profound religious truth. Yet for all that, many of the details of his early life, given in the oldest sources remain evocative of some memory of events from a distant time. If we persist in distinguishing and holding apart myth and history, we are in danger of missing the story's own sense of truth. Furthermore, the historian must recognise that he has virtually no strictly historical criteria for distinguishing between history and myth in the account of the life of the Buddha. And at that point he should perhaps remain silent and let the story speak for itself.'

Questions
1) What is the difference between myth and history?
2) What does Rupert Gethin mean by describing the life of the Buddha as 'an archetype'?
3) What does Rupert Gethin say we risk missing if we make a strong distinction between myth and history?

Further information for tasks set in students' book

Which is more important: the Buddha or his teaching?

Key features of this discussion might include:

Arguments in favour of the Buddha

- Without the spiritual quest of the Buddha, the path may not have been found, and there would then be no teaching.
- The Buddha's decision to teach was crucial to the development of the religion.
- The Buddha is an example and an inspiration to those on the path to enlightenment.

Arguments in favour of his teaching

- The Buddha is not a God, or an avatar, or an incarnation of the divine. There is arguably no historical necessity to his existence. He himself is not important. He is not worshipped, but venerated.
- Anyone could have found the truth about suffering and release from suffering. The truth was always there, regardless of whether anyone realised it.
- It is the teachings, and not the Buddha, which can help Buddhists attain enlightenment.

Many Buddhists emphasise the humanity of the Buddha. Some of the stories about his conception and birth seem out of keeping with this emphasis. How might these stories be explained?

Key features of this discussion might include:

- The importance of the humanity of the Buddha – he is not a god. What he achieved, we can achieve;
- Supernatural stories can be taken simply at face value. The Buddha was an extraordinary human being, with special powers that seem unlikely from our current scientific perspective, but our knowledge about what it possible is always changing;
- Supernatural stories can be understood by thinking about the purpose of the writers of the Buddha's life. How would they show he was extraordinary to people who had not been born when he lived?
- Supernatural stories can be understood by thinking about the worldviews of the writers of the Buddha's life. India at the time of the Buddha was a crucible of various religious beliefs – and supernatural powers would have been accepted as real. It would therefore be unthinkable that a man as great as the Buddha did not have them;
- The stories are pregnant with meaning. An elephant is an auspicious animal. One does not have to believe that an elephant entered Maya's womb in order to understand the meaning of associating an auspicious animal with the conception of the Buddha-to-be;
- It is interesting to note that the Buddha always taught against displaying the supernatural powers thought to arise in meditation, as doing so encourages attachment in oneself and others.

Explain the meaning for contemporary Buddhists of events in the life of the Buddha.

Additional resource for this task

The early life of the Buddha told in very accessible novel form:

http://www2.dc.net/nowk/buddha/buddha_story.html

Key features of this answer might include:

- Reference to some of the reading mentioned above;
- Awareness of the historical/mythic status of events in the life of the Buddha, and the primacy of meaning;
- Recognition of the importance of the humanity of the Buddha as illustrated, for example, by his ordinary death;
- Understanding of the allegorical nature of the Four Sights – an account designed to assist reflection on the true nature of reality and the extent to which we are unaware of it;
- The inspirational nature of the quest;
- Answers that do not merely recount events in the life of the Buddha.

'A story 2,500 years old can have no relevance for today'. Assess the validity of this view.

Key features of this answer might include:

- **Against the proposition:**

  The Buddha is an inspiration to others. Even if the account of his life is untrue, it works as a narrative, and through it it is possible to see how the true nature of reality might be understood.

- **In favour of the proposition:**

  It is for each person to work out his/her path and enlightenment him/herself. The karmic conditions in which individuals find themselves are very different from those of the Buddha. The Buddha's life story contains much supernatural material that the modern reader may find off-putting.

- **Read some of the Jataka tales. How might a Buddhist use these stories to help him/her on her own path?** (e.g. at http://www.accesstoinsight.org/lib/bps/leaves/bl135.htm or www.buddhanet.net/e-learning/buddhism/bt/conts.htm)
- **Consider the limitations of biography. Does reading a biography of a person mean you really know them? How far is it possible for biographies to be accurate?**
- **Is all history really myth?**

Opportunities for Synoptic Element preparation

It would be advisable for students to make notes in preparation for the A2 Synoptic Assessment in areas which include:

- **Religious Authority**

  The authority which the Buddha invested in his teachers for the six years of his austerities, which he was ultimately to reject in favour of the authority of his own experience.

- **Religious Experience**

  The experience of the ascetic path. The Buddha's key experience of enlightenment in the context of meditation. The nature of truth as beyond language, only to be experienced directly.

- **Life, Death and Life After Death**

  The Buddha's realisation of the inevitability of death with the third of the Four Sights. The Buddha's awareness of the rebirth of all beings during the second watch of the night. .

Chapter 3: The Buddha: A Human Example

The focus of this chapter is on the humanity of the Buddha, and the way in which devotion to his memory grew in early Buddhism. This chapter begins to explore some of the terminology used in relation to Buddhists' respect for the Buddha. Problems with the term 'worship' are introduced (this discussion arises again in Chapter 10).

Questions for revision

21. What is the Sangha?
22. What is a stupa?
23. What does Theravada mean?
24. Why do Buddhists make offerings to statues?

Answers can be found on page 48.

Further resources for the study of the Buddha as a human example can be found amongst those on his life

Cush, Denise	Buddhism	5-11
Harvey, Peter	Buddhism	4-5
Harvey, Peter	An Introduction to Buddhism: Teaching, History and Practices	9-14
Skilton, Andrew	A Concise History of Buddhism	3-18
Snelling, John	The Buddhist Handbook	3-19
Gethin, Rupert	The Foundations of Buddhism	7-13

Explore the Great Stupa at Sanchi online at
www.buddhanet.net/e-learning/history/buddhist-art/sanchi.htm

From *Buddhism*, by Denise Cush, Hodder and Stoughton, 1993 p. 45

'In Theravada teaching, the Buddha was a man, a human being like ourselves. Certainly he was the most special man who ever lived in our era because he himself, by struggling for thousands of lives, finally managed to achieve for himself the knowledge that leads to liberation. However much popular devotion ascribes special characteristics to him, such as the 32 marks of a superbeing* and his miraculous birth – it is vital not to forget that he is one of us, and we are called to achieve the state of enlightenment obtained by him. A Buddha is a very rare occurrence, and does not mean any enlightened person but only one who has achieved enlightenment by himself, and taught others. Then Buddha Shakyamuni is now dead and beyond any contact with struggling beings, as are all dead enlightened ones. However, the tradition gives us everything we need to know about what he taught when he was alive.'

Question
Why is the humanity of the Buddha important to Theravada Buddhists?

* According to ancient Indian tradition, a Buddha or a universal emperor would be born with 32 marks on his body, for example the bump on his head signifying wisdom, which identified him from birth as somebody extraordinary.

Further information for tasks set in students' book

Seminar topic p. 18   **KS/C KS/WO KS/ILP**

If Theravada Buddhists think the Buddha was just a man, why do they bow and make offerings before his statue?

Key features of this discussion might include:

- The Buddha was not 'just a man'. His attainment made him different from all other human beings. In answer to a question from a Brahmin he once denied that he was a human, because he was no longer subject to rebirth or suffering in the way that humans are. The Buddha's humanity is important in that it means what he did, we can do, but his attainment puts him into an extraordinary category;
- Buddhists bow in part for cultural reasons. Buddhism grew up in countries where bowing was a common feature of respectful human interaction;
- When Buddhists bow and make offerings they are honouring and respecting the Buddha's attainment, and demonstrating gratitude for it;
- They are also showing with their body language that they consider the Buddha to have attained something far beyond anything they have attained.

Research task p. 18   **KS/C KS/IT KS/WO KS/ILP**

Find out what happened after the death of other great religious founders. How did each religion preserve its authority? Did the founder tell his followers that they should consult a book of revelation, a book containing his own writings, or the writings of others? Did he establish a successor of any kind? In what way is the case of the Buddha similar or different?

This task is particularly recommended for those looking at 'authority' for synoptic assessment. It will require Internet research, and a range of general RS reference books, such as The Oxford Dictionary of World Religions, edited by John Bowker, Oxford OUP, 1997.

In addition to Islam, Judaism, Sikhism, Hinduism and Christianity, students can look other religions such as Jainism, Bahaism, Shinto, Confucianism, and Taoism.

Key to the success of this research task is the highlighting of what is distinctive about the way in which the Buddha invested authority in the Sangha collectively, and in the dharma ('He who sees the dharma sees me'); the way in which the teachings were passed on orally; and the way in which stupa veneration became a part of Buddhist life.

The research could be presented to the class as a PowerPoint presentation.

Extension task

Read the section entitled 'The nature of a Buddha' in Rupert Gethin's The Foundations of Buddhism OUP, 1998 p27-30.
Consider how accurate it is to describe the Buddha as 'just a man'.

Opportunities for Synoptic Element preparation

It would be advisable for students to make notes in preparation for the A2 Synoptic Assessment in areas which include:

*   **Religious Authority**
    Authority of the Buddha as a human example. Authority of the Sangha, and of the dharma.
*   **Religious Experience**
    Experience of identifying with the Buddha as a human being.
*   **Life, Death and Life After Death**
    The notion that all life is subject to death.

Chapter 4: The Buddha: A Celestial Being

This chapter expands on the meaning of the Buddha in the wider traditions of Buddhism.

It is a challenge in the study of Buddhism to give fair treatment to all of the traditions. Because the story of Siddhartha is so accessible, and because the Theravada understanding of his status appeals at a common sense level, there has been a tendency, even amongst academics (though less so nowadays), to see Theravada as a pure form of Buddhism and the life of Siddhartha as the 'gospel' of Buddhism.

At AS level, students need to be able to come to their own critical conclusions about the different traditions of Buddhism, but they should not dismiss Mahayana and Tibetan forms simply on the basis that they do not conform to the Theravada interpretation: this is only one interpretation amongst many others. Theravada may have some claim to historical primacy, but it should not therefore be celebrated as the perfect form of the religion in the same way that some Christian theologians might celebrate the Early Church. In any case, the nature of history is understood differently from a Buddhist perspective than from a Christian one.

Questions for revision

25. Name a Mahayana Philosopher.
26. What is Buddha-nature?
27. What does bodhisattva mean?
28. What are Avalokitesvara's characteristics?
29. Name the Dhyani Buddhas.
30. Explain Lin Chi's instruction 'if you see the Buddha in your path, kill him.'
31. What is the relationship between Wisdom and Compassion?

Answers can be found on page 48.

Further resources for the study of The Buddha: A Celestial Being

Cush, Denise	Buddhism	86-87
Harvey, Peter	An Introduction to Buddhism: Teaching, History and Practices (very advanced)	125-127
Skilton, Andrew	A Concise History of Buddhism	103
Snelling, John	The Buddhist Handbook	100

Research celestial Buddhas and bodhisattvas online at
www.buddhanet.net/e-learning/history/deities.htm

From *Buddhism* by Denise Cush, Hodder & Stoughton, 1993 p. 84

Some features of Mahayana Buddhism

'Mahayana Buddhists speak of Bodhisattvas as heavenly beings with the power to help those who call on them. These bodhisattvas have their own names, characteristics and iconography and may appear in visions or be the focus of meditation. Some of the more well known are Avalokitesvara, Manjusri, Maitreya, Kshitigarbha and Tara.

The Mahayana universe – or multiverse – is even larger than the cosmology of the Theravada Buddhists. In addition to this world system, with its three realms of sense desire, form and formlessness, there are other world systems, in which may dwell other Buddhas than the Shakyamuni Buddha of this world system. Among the more well known of these Buddhas are Amitabha, Akshobhya, and Vairocana. Like the bodhisattvas, some of whom share their worlds, the cosmic Buddhas may appear in visions, be the focus of meditations or be asked for help.

According to some Mahayana scriptures Shakyamuni Buddha, the Buddha of our world system is available in a glorious, heavenly or spiritual form, like the other Buddhas and bodhisattvas.

For some Mahayana Buddhists, especially in Chinese and Japanese traditions, the word Buddha no longer refers to particular beings, whether earthly or heavenly, but to the ultimate reality underlying the whole universe, everywhere and in everyone.'

Questions
1) **Name some Buddhas.**
2) **Name some bodhisattvas.**
3) **How is Shakyamuni Buddha understood in Mahayana Buddhism?**
4) **What does Denise Cush mean when she says the word Buddha has come to refer to the ultimate reality underlying the whole universe?**

Further information for tasks set in students' book

Explain the different ways that the concept of 'Buddha' is understood within Buddhism.

Key features of this answer might include:

- Reference to some of the writers mentioned above;
- Explanation of the following:
  - The understanding of the 'historical' Buddha as a human example to those on the path
  - The founder of the religion
  - One of the three jewels and refuges
  - The title given to any enlightened being
  - The role of the celestial or cosmic Buddhas
  - The principle of enlightenment of which all enlightened beings are instances, and the potentiality of all beings (buddha-nature)
  - The underlying nature of all reality.

Evaluate the view that the Mahayana understanding of buddhahood is a corruption of proper Buddhism.

Arguments in favour of the proposition might include:

- The Buddha was a 'one off'. Other enlightened beings have relied on his teachings to become enlightened. He enlightened himself. So there is only one Buddha in our reality. This is the Theravada view;
- The Mahayana Scriptures were not agreed by the Council of the Sangha. They developed independently according to a wide variety of schools of thought;
- Any enlightened state takes lifetimes to attain. To say that anyone, no matter how bound by craving and attachment they are, is a potential Buddha may seem to belittle its status.

Arguments against the proposition might include:

- How might a definition of 'proper' Buddhism be reached? Is a religion 'proper' when it is closest to the teachings of its founder (if those are truly known), or is a religion 'proper' when it makes modern relevant reinterpretations of the teachings so that people can accept them?
- How might a definition of 'corruption' be reached? Is corruption a watering down of teachings? Has the Mahayana tradition watered down the core teachings of Buddhism, or just expressed them differently for the Theravada?
- Could the most important criterion be whether the teachings help people to overcome suffering and reach nirvana?

Extension task

Research the doctrine of the three bodies of the Buddha. (Gethin pp. 231-234)

- **What new information about the concept of 'buddha' does this doctrine introduce?**
- **How does it help clarify the Mahayana belief in a great pantheon of bodhisattvas and buddhas?**

Opportunities for Synoptic Element preparation

It would be advisable for students to make notes in preparation for the A2 Synoptic Assessment in areas which include:

- **Religious Authority**

  The wide range of authorities in Buddhism, from the historical Buddha to the pantheon of Buddhas and Bodhisattvas. In understanding these cosmic enlightened beings, Buddhists find authority for the virtues and positive qualities that they try to develop in themselves. The cosmic Buddhas are authoritative representations of features of enlightenment.

- **Religious Experience**

  The transformative experience of visualisation of cosmic enlightened beings in meditation (e.g. Catherine's experience on page 22 of the students' book).

- **Life, Death and Life After Death**

  The notion that there are many realms additional to the human realm.

Chapter 5: The Three Marks of Existence and the Four Noble Truths

These concepts, though abstract, are relatively easy to learn by rote. What distinguishes the level five from the level two and three answers is the evidence that students have understood these concepts in their own way, and can use their own words to express and explain them. Questions that have 'explain' as a trigger word often trip up unwary students, who merely express doctrines formulaically without any attempt to demonstrate their understanding of them. This can be done with the use of examples and illustrations, with commentary, personal reflections, and a sense of questioning personal engagement with the material learnt.

Questions for revision

32. What is dukkha?
33. What is anicca?
34. What is anatta?
35. What are pretas?
36. What does the parable of the poisoned arrow illustrate?
37. Why can the Buddha not be described as an eternalist?
38. What central Buddhist doctrine does Nagasena illustrate with his metaphor of the chariot?
39. What is the Middle Way?

Answers can be found on pages 48-49.

Further resources for the study of the Three Marks of Existence and the Four noble Truths

Cush, Denise	Buddhism	27-39
Harvey, Peter	Buddhism	75-84
Harvey, Peter	An Introduction to Buddhism: Teaching, History and Practices	47-72
Clarke and Thompson	Buddhism: A New Approach	19-23
Keown, Damien	Buddhism: A Very Short Introduction	43-55

Reading

Adapted from Peter Harvey (ed) *Buddhism*, Continuum, 2001 p76

'i) Birth is dukkha, ageing is dukkha, sickness is dukkha, death is dukkha,

ii) Sorrow, lamentation, pain, grief and despair are dukkha,

iii) Association with what one dislikes is dukkha, separation from what one likes is dukkha, not to get what one wants is dukkha,

iv) Identifying any of the skandhas as self is dukkha.

The first five features described as dukkha are basic biological aspects of being alive, each of which can be painful and traumatic. The dukkha here is compounded by the rebirth perspective of Buddhism, for this involves repeated rebirth, re-aging, re-sickness and re-death. The second set of features refers to physical or mental pain that arises from the vicissitudes of life. The third set of features points to the fact that we can never wholly succeed in keeping away things, people, and situations that we dislike, in holding on to those we do like or in getting what we want. The changing, unstable nature of life is such that we are led to experience dissatisfaction, loss and disappointment – in a word, frustration.

Is Buddhism 'pessimistic' in emphasising the unpleasant aspects of life? A Buddhist's reply is that the transcending of suffering requires a fully realistic assessment of its pervasive presence in life. One must accept that one is 'ill' if a cure is to be possible; ignoring the problem only makes it worse. The path to the end of suffering, moreover, is one in which the deep calm and joy of devotion and meditation play an important part. Buddhism, then, does not deny the existence of happiness in the world – it provides ways of increasing it – but it does emphasise that all forms of happiness (bar that of nirvana) do not last. Sooner or later, they slip through one's fingers and leave an aftertaste of loss and longing – thus even happiness is to be seen as dukkha. This can be more clearly understood when one considers another classification of states of dukkha; dukkha as physical pain, dukkha due to change, and the dukkha of conditioned phenomena. When a happy feeling passes it often leads to dukkha due to change, and, even while it is occurring, it is dukkha in the sense of being a limited, conditioned, imperfect state – one which is not truly satisfactory. This most subtle sense of dukkha is sometimes experienced in feelings of vague unease at the fragility and transitoriness of life.'

Questions
1) **What is dukkha?**
2) **Why does change result in dukkha?**
3) **Why is happiness considered to be dukkha?**
4) **Is Buddhism pessimistic? Explain your answer.**

Further information for tasks set in students' book

Explain how the parable of the poisoned arrow illustrates possible distractions from the quest for enlightenment.

Key features of this answer might include:
- An accurate account of the parable of the poisoned arrow;
- An explanation of the nature of the quest for enlightenment;
- An explanation of the types of distractions from the path of enlightenment, the persistence of the three fires, attachment to the idea of self, fruitless speculation about issues such as the creation of the universe, the destination of individuals after death and whether life after death is eternal;
- An explanation of the way in which the parable highlights the absurdity of such speculation, and the urgency of our current situation, immersed in suffering as we are, and the way in which we fail to recognise help when it is at hand.

'Buddhists are wrong when they say that questions about creation and life after death are merely speculation.' Assess the validity of this view. Present your findings to the rest of the class.

Arguments in favour of the proposition might include:
- Many religions teach that God created the world and that life after death is a certain hope;
- Science can tell us much about the origins of the universe;
- Many people believe that phenomena such as near-death experiences and spirit medium-ship etc. are evidence of life after death;
- Many people would argue that questions about creation and life after death are amongst the most important questions humans can ask. If we had the answers to those, we may know the 'meaning of life'.

Arguments against the proposition might include:
- Some people believe that we will never have final answers to questions such as these, so they question the point of speculating about them;
- There are many other pressing questions that humans could more usefully attempt to answer, such as how to cure cancer and AIDS, how to beat world poverty, how to bring peace to war-torn areas of the world, etc.;
- Buddhists often say that asking such questions is not helpful at all in developing non-attachment. Answers to such questions or views about the nature of the universe can become objects of attachment in themselves, and answers (were it possible to have them!) would not help in the quest for enlightenment.

In your group, read today's edition of a broadsheet newspaper.

Pick out any examples of what Buddhists might consider a deluded attachment to self, and comment on them.

Advertisements that appeal to our vanity are easy examples. More difficult are news stories that show the participants clinging to a particular world view. Be aware that not all conflict necessarily involves attachment to self or false views. Many people in this world, including Buddhists, campaign against oppression of many different kinds.

Opportunities for Synoptic Element preparation

It would be advisable for students to make notes in preparation for the A2 Synoptic Assessment in areas which include:

- **Religious Authority**

  The authority of the Dharma – the Buddha's teaching on the Four Truths and the Three Marks. The authority of experience. The Buddha did not ask his followers to have faith in these teachings, but to test them out for themselves.

- **Religious Experience**

  The Buddha's own experience of the truth of the Four Truths and the Three Marks. The experience of these truths in the lives of Buddhists. The importance of experience rather than faith.

- **Life, Death and Life After Death**

  The tendency in Buddhism to avoid speculation about the nature of life after death, where you are likely to be reborn, whether life after death is eternal, whether a Buddha exists after death, etc.

Chapter 6: Rebirth and Interconnectedness

This chapter explores the notion of karma; how the intentions of an action are either wholesome or unwholesome; and how those intentions have an inevitable effect. It also explores the connected nature of reality, as depicted in the Wheel of Life.

Questions for revision

40. What is karma?
41. What is anatta?
42. What is the Bhavacakra?
43. What is Pratitya Samutpada?
44. What is the difference between rebirth and reincarnation?
45. What are the six realms?
46. How is ignorance symbolised in the first of the twelve links?
47. Explain the symbolism of the hungry ghost.
48. Explain why the three fires/poisons are depicted at the hub of the wheel.

Answers can be found on page 49.

Further resources for the study of rebirth and interconnectedness

Cush, Denise	Buddhism	29-31
Clarke &Thompson	Buddhism: A New Approach	29-32
Harvey, Peter	An Introduction to Buddhism: Teaching, History and Practices	37-46
Snelling, John	The Buddhist Handbook	69-78

Read the Dhammapada online at
www.buddhanet.net/e-learning/buddhism/dp01.htm

From *The Buddhist Handbook* by John Snelling, Rider, 1987 p72

Rebirth

'Closely linked to the notion of karma is that of rebirth. This should not be confused with reincarnation, which is the view that there is a soul or subtle essence imprinted with an enduring personal stamp that transmigrates or commutes from body to body down through the aeons. Buddhism of course rejects that view. What it does admit, however, is a causal connection between one life and another. Thus the karmic accumulations, good and bad, of a particular life (itself the culmination of an endless series of causally connected past lives) will condition a new birth. Sequences of such interconnected lives form a continuum. Nothing is handed on, however, but the conditioning: the influences, the karmic charge.

To clarify this notion various standard illustrations have been developed. There is this example of the flame that is passed from one candle to others. It is not exactly the same flame that carries on down the line, but it is not a different one either. Another is the cannoning of billiard balls. One ball strikes another; on impact it stops dead; but the other ball moves on, strikes another ball and itself stops dead; then a third ball continues the process.... It is a single movement, passed on through a sequence of temporary vehicles.

It must stressed that rebirth isn't just something which bridges the abyss between one physical life and another. It is something that is happening all the time. As we've already noted, our bodies are undergoing minute cellular changes from moment to moment; our feelings and thoughts change too. What appear to be then our continuous, flowing lives, are in reality sequences of essentially separate life moments, each a death and a rebirth. Take the analogy of a film. It is made up of individual frames each slightly different from the next. As the film is run through a projector, however, the frames blend into each other and illusion of flow is created. Our fascination with the ongoing drama obscures the true nature of what is happening.'

Questions
1) **Explain the analogy of the flame.**
2) **Explain the analogy of the billiard balls.**
3) **Explain the analogy of the filmstrip.**
4) **The point of Snelling's last sentence - 'Our fascination with the ongoing drama obscures the true nature of what its happening' - is that it could be said as much for life as for a film script. Explain why.**

Further information for tasks set in students' book

Writing task p. 43 KS/C KS/ILP

Explain the Buddhist understanding of the six realms.

Key features of this answer might include:

- Reference to some of the reading mentioned above;
- Correct identification and description of each realm, the gods, the jealous gods, the animals, the hells, the hungry ghosts and the human realm;
- Understanding that no realm, not even the hells or the realms of the gods, are permanent or eternal;
- Understanding of the symbolism of the iconography e.g. hungry ghosts;
- Understanding of the demythologised understanding of the realms, that they represent states of mind;
- The meaning of the presence of the Buddha in each of them.

Writing task p. 43 KS/C KS/PS KS/ILP

Assess the view that Buddhists believe in life after death.

Arguments in favour of the proposition might include:

- Widespread belief in rebirth in the Buddhist world;
- Belief in reincarnated lamas in Tibetan Buddhism (life before birth implying life after death);
- Japanese belief in a Pure Land.

Arguments against the proposition might include:

- No life after death in the sense that an atman is reborn into another life;
- The Buddha did not encourage speculation about the nature of life after death;
- The Buddha gave no information on whether a Buddha would exist after death;
- Theravada tradition of seeing the Buddha as inaccessible since his parinirvana.

Additional resource for this task

For further material on the Wheel of Becoming, explore the iconography online at:

http://easyweb.easynet.co.uk/~pt/Buddhism/books/wheel

Extension task 1 KS/C KS/PS KS/ILP

Buddhists often suggest that we should relate to all beings as if they were our mother. The belief in rebirth means that quite possibly anyone or any being we encounter could have been our mother in some lifetime.

Consider the practical implications of thinking in this way, and consider how doing so might assist Buddhists in realising the truth of Pratitya Samutpada.

Extension task 2

John Snelling in 'The Buddhist Handbook p74-75, describes the rebuke that Ananda, the Buddha's cousin and closest disciple, received when he boldly told the Buddha that he had understood the doctrine of Pratitya Samutpada:

'Say not so, Ananda, say not so! Deep is this doctrine of events as arising from causes …. It is through not understanding this doctrine, through not penetrating it, that this generation has become a tangled skein, a matted ball of thread, lie to munja-grass and rushes, unable to overpass the doom of the Waste, the Woeful Way, the Downfall, the Constant Round of Transmigration.' (from the Mahanidana Suttanta)

Why is Pratitya Samutpada so difficult to understand? What is it about the way human beings think and behave that makes it so?

Extension task 3

There are slight differences in the way the bhavacakra is depicted in different traditions of Buddhism and by different artists. The bhavacakra in the students' handbook on p. 39 is painted by an artist who paints in a Tibetan tradition. Some pictures of the bhavacakra show a Buddha in every realm. Why do you think this is?

Opportunities for Synoptic Element preparation

It would be advisable for students to make notes in preparation for the A2 Synoptic Assessment in areas which include:

- **Religious Authority**
  The authority of the teachings of rebirth and Pratitya Samutpada, that need to be understood individually by each person. The psychological reality of the realms of rebirth.
- **Religious Experience**
  Experience of the realisation of interconnectedness and rebirth. The experience of iconography as didactic inspiration.
- **Life, Death and Life After Death**
  The notion of samsara, different reams of existence, the understanding of the realms as having a psychological reality as well as being possible rebirth destinations.

Chapter 7: The Eightfold Path

The Noble Eightfold path is easy to learn and to describe. Students find it less easy to explain its elements, and how they each contribute to Buddhist life and to the quest for enlightenment.

Questions for revision

49. What is panna?
50. What is sila?
51. What is samadhi?
52. What is dana?
53. What are the paramitas?
54. How does the Eightfold Path help Buddhists to tread the 'Middle Way'?

Answers can be found on page 50.

Further resources for the study of the Eightfold Path

Cush, Denise	Buddhism	33-35
Clarke & Thompson,	Buddhism: A new approach	24-25
Skilton, Andrew	A Concise History of Buddhism	31-35
Snelling, John	The Buddhist Handbook	55-63
Keown, Damien	Buddhism: A Very Short Introduction	53-55

Reading

From *Buddhism: A Very Short Introduction* by Damien Keown, OUP, 1996 p53-55

'The Eightfold Path is known as the 'Middle Way' because it steers a course between a life of indulgence and one of harsh austerity. It consists of eight factors divided in the three categories of Morality, Meditation, Wisdom. These define the parameters of human good and indicate where the scope for human flourishing lies…

Although the Path consists of eight factors, they should not be thought of as stages which are passed through on the way to nirvana then left behind. Instead, the eight factors exemplify the ways in which morality, meditation, and wisdom are to be cultivated on a continuing basis. Right View [Understanding] means first, the acceptance of Buddhist teachings and later their experiential confirmation. Right Resolve [Thought] means making a serious commitment to developing right attitudes. Right Speech means telling the truth and speaking in a thoughtful and sensitive way. Right Action means abstaining from wrongful bodily behaviour such as killing, stealing, or behaving wrongfully with respect to sensual pleasures. Right Livelihood means not engaging in an occupation which causes harm to others. Right Effort means gaining control of one's thoughts and cultivating positive states of mind. Right Mindfulness means cultivating constant awareness, and Right Meditation means developing deep levels of mental calm through various techniques which concentrate the mind and integrate the personality.

In this respect the practice of the Eightfold Path is a kind of modelling process: the eight factors reveal how a Buddha would live, and by living like a Buddha one gradually becomes one. The Eightfold Path is thus a path of self-transformation: an intellectual, emotional, and moral restructuring in which a person is re-oriented from selfish limited objectives toward a horizon of possibilities and opportunities for fulfilment. Through the pursuit of knowledge (panna) and moral virtue (sila), ignorance and selfish desire are overcome, the cause of the arising of suffering is removed, and nirvana is attained.'

Questions
1) **Why is the Eightfold Path known as the Middle Way?**
2) **Why does Damien Keown describe the Eightfold Path as a kind of modelling process?**
3) **Why shouldn't the Eightfold Path be thought of as a series of steps or stages?**
4) **What does Damien Keown mean when he describes the path as one of self transformation?**

Further information for tasks set in students' book

Seminar topic p. 47

KS/C KS/WO KS/ILP

Can you see any substantial difference between the paramitas and the Eightfold Path?

Key features of this discussion might include:

- The addition of Giving, Energy and Patience – though these could be understood as part of Right Action, Right Effort and Right Mindfulness;

- Theravada Buddhists also refer to the paramitas as 'factors of enlightenment', and Mahayana Buddhists also sometimes refer to ten paramitas instead of six. It is not possible to draw clear distinctions between the qualities valued in Mahayana and Theravada Buddhism. They have much in common.

Writing task p. 48

KS/C KS/ILP

Explain the practical teachings of Buddhism designed to overcome craving and attachment.

Key features of this answer might include:

- Reference to some of the reading recommended above;

- Some consideration of the term practical: the Buddha taught things to do and to try, attitudes to experiment with, and so on, as means to ends. The effects of these practices could only be known experientially;

- Consideration of the way in which the teaching of the Four Noble Truths may lead to an intellectual realisation of the causes of suffering and unsatisfactoriness;

- Consideration of the eight factors of the Eightfold Path, and/or the paramitas, and/or the ten stages of the bodhisattva path, and the kind of attitudes and behaviour they are designed to combat and the virtues in which they will result. These virtues are not sought for their own sake but because they provide the foundation of enlightenment;

- A sense of awareness that the teachings are not commandments but that trying to live in a certain way with an awareness of the causes of constant rebirth into the wheel of samsara can help develop detachment and ultimately liberation.

Chapter 7

'Living a religious life is much more to do with what you believe than following rules.' Evaluate this view.

Key features of this answer might include:
- Consideration of more than one point of view.

Arguments in favour of the proposition might include:

There is much evidence in many religions that belief is considered more important than the slavish and self-interested following of rules.

- The Reformation in Christianity for example, emphasised 'faith' over 'works';
- Jesus spoke out against keeping the letter of the law for its own sake;
- In Buddhism the Dharma is not seen as a set of rules to follow, but as a path worth experimenting with if the overcoming of craving and attachment is your goal.

Arguments against the proposition might include:

The Buddha taught his followers not to 'believe' anything blindly or accept anything on the authority of anyone or anything other than their own experience. Arguably, Buddhism cannot be associated with either 'beliefs' or 'the following of rules' (except in the context of the pattimokka rules for the Theravada monastic Sangha);

- Many religions do emphasise the careful keeping of rules or traditions, for example the laws of Kashrut in Judaism, but these are usually for reasons related to beliefs (for example about the Sovereignty of God) and are not merely regulations.

Consider the precept of abstaining from the misuse of speech, and the Right Speech factor of the Eightfold Path (the precepts are studied on page 51 of the student text).

Explore newspapers, TV, Internet and other media to discover the ways that modern culture fails to use Right Speech. Find evidence of the consequences of this. Remember that Right Speech is not only about not lying, it is about avoiding angry or argumentative speech, it is about avoiding gossip, or idle and frivolous speech, in fact any speech which is not conducive to enlightenment.

Pool your findings with the others in your group, and present your view of a modern society that used right speech to the class.

Opportunities for Synoptic Element preparation

It would be advisable for students to make notes in preparation for the A2 Synoptic Assessment in areas which include:

- **Religious Authority**

  The experiential authority of the dharma.

- **Religious Experience**

  Experience of liberation from craving and attachment of those who try to practise the Eightfold Path, or the bodhisattva path.

- **Life, Death and Life After Death**

  The idea that life in samsara continues as a result of craving and attachment, but that there are practical measures that can be taken to defeat craving and attachment, thus leading to liberation and nirvana.

Chapter 8: The Sangha

The Sangha provides the context for Buddhist practice. Students should be aware of its importance as one of the three jewels and refuges, and of the conventions and precepts which regulate it. They should understand the role of community in a religion that is sometimes presented as individualistic and personal in the west.

Questions for revision

55. What are the three jewels?
56. What is the Sangha?
57. What is going for refuge?
58. What are the precepts?
59. What is merit?
60. What are the monastic precepts?
61. What is the Vinaya Pitaka
62. Explain the importance of the 'Three Jewels' in Buddhism'.

Answers can be found on page 50.

Further resources for the study of the Sangha

Cush, Denise	*Buddhism*	57-59, 81-84 & 72-75
Clarke & Thompson	*Buddhism: A new appraoch*	33-43
Harvey, Peter	*An Introduction to Buddhism: Teaching, History and Practices*	217-243
Skilton, Andrew	*A Concise History of Buddhism*	39-43
Gethin, Rupert	*The Foundations of Buddhism*	85-111

From *The Foundations of Buddhism* by Rupert Gethin, OUP, 1998 p 85-86

'The basis of the renouncer's lifestyle lies in two things: (1) renunciation of the household life for the sake of the religious life, and (2) dependence upon the generosity of the population at large for the provision of material needs – food, clothing, and dwellings. The success of early Buddhism thus assumes both a desire on the part of certain members of the population to give up 'normal society' or the household life and sufficient good will on the part of those remaining in normal society to allow them to do so. The followers of a teacher such as the Buddha thus fell into two socially distinct categories: homeless wanderers and lay supporters.

Buddhists have, then, always understood the Buddha's message not only as an invitation to give up the household life and join the Buddha's group of monks, but also as an invitation to the wider community to support the religious life. The Buddhist understanding of the nature of the life-style of "one gone forth" sees the Buddhist monastic community as a significant part of society as a whole. Thus when the Buddha is reported, shortly after his awakening, as instructing his growing group of newly "awakened" monastic followers to set off, never two by the same way to teach Dharma that is "lovely in the beginning, lovely the middle, lovely in the end", "For the benefit and happiness of the many, out of sympathy for the world, for the good, benefit, and happiness of gods and men", this represents more than simply a recruitment drive for the Sangha or Order of Monks and Nuns. The presence of Buddhist monks and nuns within a society has been seen as in itself a positive good and of benefit for all.'

Questions

1) **What does Rupert Gethin say are the two bases of the life of renouncers (the monastic Sangha)?**
2) **Why is the monastic Sangha 'a significant part of society as a whole', and why is the presence of the monastic Sangha seen as in itself a positive good and benefit for all?**

Further information for tasks set in students' book

Explain why renunciation of worldly life might be considered helpful on the path to enlightenment?

Key features of this answer might include:

- Reference to some of the reading mentioned above;
- An awareness that renunciation, but not overt austerities, is valued in Buddhism;
- The monastic Sangha lives a life largely without possessions, helping them to develop detachment from material things;
- They live without responsibility for feeding their families or themselves, therefore do not have to work for money, or be tied to money in anyway. In fact they take a precept to refrain from handling money at all;
- They are free from the pressures of modern life in the outside world, such as the pressure to succeed in one's career, or to live at the mercy of advertising, the stock market etc.;
- They are free from sexual and romantic distractions;
- They have a great deal of time for meditation and for study, and more time and opportunity than those in the outside world to really contemplate the human condition;
- They have the opportunity to teach others;
- Renunciation might be considered helpful because the Buddha himself lived the life of renunciation, and might encourage those who wanted to seek nirvana to do the same.

Assess the view that monastic life is escapist, as it does not engage with the real world.

Key features of this answer might include:

- Consideration of more than one point of view;
- Monks and nuns do live a life free from the responsibilities and stresses of the life of the outside world. Monasteries only exist where the lay people are willing to support the community with gifts of food and other necessities, so they are by nature supported communities;
- Sometimes monastic communities have been criticised for becoming too 'closed' to the problems of the outside world. However, often Sangha members have had experience of life before they renounced, so they know the pressures of the real world, and can teach in ways relevant to the lay people;
- Even when this is not the case, the life of those living in the outside world could be seen as escapist, and full of distractions from the problems of sickness, old age and death, and the causes of imprisonment in the cycle of becoming. Only in the monastery are these fully faced, and only in the monastery is there no escape from them into reading or TV, socialising, sex, partying, alcohol, shopping or drugs. There is not even the option of burying oneself in one's work! The question of the meaning of life has to be faced full-on;
- This is part of the reason why the Sangha is considered to be venerable and worthy of gifts – because its members do the difficult things that lay-people need not do.

The Sangha is sometimes described as 'a field of merit'. What does this mean?
(See Peter Harvey, *An Introduction to Buddhism: Teaching, History and Practices* p. 198-9)

Extension task 2 KS/C KS/IT KS/PS KS/WO KS/ILP

Using the Internet or the Buddhist directory published annually by the Buddhist Society, create a map of the Buddhist groups and Sanghas in your county or region.

You should colour-code the different types and create a key to your map. You could also write to the Sanghas to ask for a profile of their members (Are they university students? Are they members of a Thai or a Japanese community living in a city? Are they British converts? Have many of them made a formal commitment to Buddhism or do they just attend meditation from time to time for other reasons?).

Opportunities for Synoptic Element preparation

It would be advisable for students to make notes in preparation for the A2 Synoptic Assessment in areas which include:

- **Religious Authority**
  The democratic nature of the Sangha and the authority of the Vinaya as a code of conduct.
  The authority of the precepts, not as rules, but as assertions of intent and aspiration.
- **Religious Experience**
  Experience of renunciation in the context of the monastic Sangha.
- **Life, Death and Life After Death**
  The notion that having been born into a situation in which it is possible to spend part of life, or even all of one's life, in a monastic setting is the fruition of positive karma from this life and from former lives.

Chapter 9: Meditation

Students at AS level should be able to see beyond the health benefits of meditation. One of the main features of answers on meditation that fail to score in the higher levels, is that Buddhists meditate to get away from the pressure of daily life and to combat stress. Whilst 'calmness' of mind is one of the objectives of many types of meditation, it is wrong to reduce meditation to mere relaxation – it puts it on a par with a nice cup of tea or an aromatherapy bath!

Questions for revision

63. What is Samatha?
64. What is Vipassana?
65. What is Zazen?
66. What is metta bhavana?
67. What are the Brahmaviharas?
68. Explain the Pure Land Buddhist attitude to meditation.

Answers can be found on pages 50-51.

Further resources for the study of meditation

Cush, Denise	*Buddhism*	59-64
Clarke & Thompson	*Buddhism: A new approach*	43-54
Harvey, Peter	*An Introduction to Buddhism: Teaching, History and Practices* (v. advanced)	244-279
Keown, Damien	*Buddhism: A Very Short Introduction*	83-95
Gethin, Rupert	*The Foundations of Buddhism* (v. advanced)	174-201

From *Buddhism: A Very Short Introduction* by Damien Keown, OUP, 1996 p. 92-94

'In insight meditation, the meditator examines every aspect of his subjective experience, breaking this down into four categories: the body and its physical sensations; feelings; mood; and mental patterns and thoughts. A typical session might proceed by extending awareness of the rise and fall of the breath to the rest of the body. Every minor sensation would be noted such as twinges, aches, itches and the impulse to move and scratch. The meditator does not respond to these impulses since the purpose of the exercise is to note with bare attention how bodily sensations arise and subside without reacting to them in the normal semi-automatic way. By learning to observe without becoming involved, the pattern of stimulus-response which underlies much human behaviour can be broken. Little by little the realisation dawns that one is free to choose how to react in all situations regardless which buttons are pushed. The grip of long-standing habits and compulsions is weakened and replaced with a new sense of freedom. The analysis is gradually extended to the whole body, the intellect being wielded like a surgeon's scalpel to dissect the various bodily parts and functions. From this the awareness arises that the body is nothing more than a temporary assemblage of bones, nerves, and tissues, certainly not a worthy object to become infatuated with or excessively attached to.

Next, attention is directed to whatever feelings arise. Pleasant and unpleasant feelings are noted as they arise and pass away. This sharpens the perception of impermanence and gives rise to the knowledge that even those things which seem most intimate to us − such as our emotions- are transient states which come and go. Next, the subject's current mood and the constant fluctuations in its overall quality and tone are observed, and finally the stream of thoughts which passes through the mind. The meditator must resist the temptation to lose himself in the daydreams and fantasies which inevitably arise. Instead, he simply observes with detachment as the thoughts and images follow one another, regarding them like clouds passing across a clear blue sky, or bubbles floating to the top of a glass. From this detached observation it gradually becomes clear that even one's conscious mind is but a process like everything else. Most people regard their mental life as their true inner essence (one thinks of Descartes' famous statement 'I think therefore I am'), but insight meditation discloses that the stream of consciousness is just one more facet of the complex interaction of the five facets of individuality, and not what one 'really is'.

The realization that there is no hidden subject who is the owner of these various sensations, feelings, moods, and ideas, and that all that exists are the experiences themselves, is the transformative insight which triggers enlightenment. The recognition that there is ultimately no subject that 'has' desires weakens and finally destroys craving once and for all, making it 'like a palm-tree whose roots have been destroyed, never to grow again'. Experientially, it is as if a great burden has been lifted: the clamourings of the ego, with its vanities, illusions, cravings and disappointments, are silenced. The result is not some kind of Stoic passivity, for emotion is not suppressed but merely freed from the distorting gravitational pull of the ego. Others begin to come more fully within one's emotional horizon as the merry-go-round of selfish craving and gratification slows and stops, to be replaced by a deep and lasting sense of peace and contentment.'

Questions
1   Why does a meditator not respond to itches and aches?
2   How is normal human behaviour changed by the practice of insight (Vipassana) meditation?
3   Why are thoughts and images which arise during meditation to be seen as 'clouds passing across a clear blue sky', or 'bubbles floating to the top of a glass'?
4   How is the teaching of anatta realised in insight meditation?
5   Why do 'others' (other people) enter one's 'emotional horizon' − (How does Insight meditation help the meditator to care more about others?)

Further information for tasks set in students' book

Explain how Buddhists meditate.

Key features of this answer might include:

- Reference to some of the reading mentioned above;
- An awareness of a range of practices within the diversity of Buddhism. Meditation can be practiced by individuals, or by groups;
- The setting of meditation: somewhere quiet, perhaps a shrine room (the Buddha mediated under a tree);
- The use of objects of contemplation - statues of the Buddha or other enlightened beings, flowers, candle flames, stones, bodhi-trees, skulls, bones, and the use of a bell for timing purposes;
- A posture which is alert but relaxed (either sitting walking, standing or lying down);
  Often there is a focussing on breathing, or on the sensations in the body, or on a mantra;
- If the meditator becomes distracted he/she will gently bring his/her thoughts back to the object of meditation;
- Particular meditations might take place, such as the metta bhavana, or the kind of analysis of the insubstantiality of things, which is the aim of Vipassana;
- In some traditions experienced meditators report different levels of absorption, or jhanas, and the way that they move through these levels;
- Some traditions advocate the use of visualisation of celestial enlightened beings, in order to help the qualities of that being become developed in oneself;
- Meditation is understood in some traditions to be something that permeates every activity in life, and is not something set aside for particular times.

Meditation is more likely to reinforce someone's sense of self than to undermine it. Assess the validity of this view.

Key features of this answer might include:

- Consideration of more than one point for view;
- Meditation can seem from the outside as rather self-indulgent activity, which has few results other than decreased stress-levels in the person who is meditating;
- Pure Land Buddhists argue that the practice of meditation is dangerous because it can reinforce one's sense of self, and a sense of religious pride about one's practice;
- However, Buddhists often dedicate the merit of their meditation practice for the benefit of others;
- The purpose of many forms of meditation is to analyse the insubstantiality of the ego, so rather than reinforcing a sense of self, mediation dismantles it;
- Like any form of religious practice, meditation is open to abuse and misunderstanding.

Additional resources for this task

The following websites will be helpful:

The Vipassana Trust: www.vipassana.com

The Samatha Trust: www.samatha.demon.co.uk

Zazen: www.mro.org/zmm/zazen.shtml

Metta bhavana as taught by Ven Sujiva www.buddhanet.net/metta_sb.htm

Extension task	KS/C KS/PS KS/WO KS/ILP

Interview a meditator to find out what they experience. Compile a detailed report, being careful to note anything that they find difficult to describe.

Your interview should glean information about what tradition of meditation the person follows, whether they have had any teachers, how long they have been practising it, whether they use any objects or visualisations, how often they do it, how they feel it has affected their life.

Opportunities for Synoptic Element preparation

It would be advisable for students to make notes in preparation for the A2 Synoptic Assessment in areas which include:

- **Religious Authority**

  Authority of the various traditions of meditation practice, many of which come from before the Buddha's time. The anti-authority stance of Zen meditation practice.

- **Religious Experience**

  Experience as the key feature of Buddhist meditation. Meditation is not a theory but a practice, and can arguably only be understood if it is done on a regular basis. It is understood individually.

- **Life, Death and Life After Death**

  Buddhists sometimes meditate on death, as a focus for realising the transience of all living things. They may focus on a dying flower, or a skull, or a decomposing corpse.

Chapter 10: Puja

Students should be aware of the diversity of types of puja found in Buddhism. They should also have reflected on the complexities of describing such activities as worship.

Questions for revision

69. What is a mudra?
70. What is a mantra?
71. What is a mandala?
72. What is puja?
73. Why do some Buddhists chant the mantra Om mani padme hum?
74. Why are mandalas sometimes washed away?

Answers can be found on page 51.

Further resources for the study of puja

Harvey, Peter	Buddhism	125-149
Harvey, Peter	An Introduction to Buddhism: Teaching, History and Practices	172-190
Clarke & Thompson	Buddhism: A new approach	51,95, 81,110
Gethin, Rupert	The Foundations of Buddhism	7-13

Research puja on line at
www.buddhanet.net/e-learning/history/observances/htm
www.buddhanet.net/e-learning/history/devotion/index/htm

From *Buddhism*, edited by Peter Harvey, Continuum, 2001 p. 135-136

'In all schools of Buddhism, chanting is very common as a vehicle for devotion or other ceremonial acts and, indeed, is the most common form of meditation – i.e., practice to generate certain mind-states – in most traditions. Its use derives from early Buddhism, when Indian society made little use of writing, and a learned person was 'much-heard' rather than 'well-read'. Chanting aided accurate memory of the Buddha's teachings, as it has a rhythm which encourages the mind to flow on from word to word, and lacks melody, which might demand that the sound of some words be distorted. It is also a public medium so that errors of memory could be known and corrected. After the teachings were written down, it was still thought better that they be well memorised, and chanting had also become part of devotional life.

Buddhist chanting is neither singing nor a monotonous dirge. While being deep-toned and slightly solemn, it holds the interest with its small variations of pitch and rhythm. It is particularly impressive when a group of monks chant, for they may use different keys, all blending into a harmonious whole. The chants are usually in ancient languages, such as Pali or Old Tibetan, thus giving them an added air of sanctity. This, plus their sound quality and accompanying thoughts, generates a mixture of uplifting joy, often felt as a glow of warmth in the chest, and contemplative calm. Such states tend to arise even in those listening to a chant, if they do so with a relaxed but attentive mind. Thus monks and nuns can transmit something of the tranquillity of their way of life when chanting for the laity. Many monks know the full meaning of the chants, as they know the relevant language to some extent, and can explain them to the laity. Vernacular chants also exist.

In all traditions the most common chants are short verbal formulae, which may be strung together or repeated to form longer continuous chants. A very common [Theravadin] chant honouring Gotama Buddha is Namo Tassa Bhagavato, Arahato, Samasambuddhassa, "Honour to the Lord, Arahat, perfectly and completely Enlightened One!" This is repeated three times, and is usually followed by the chanted avowal of commitment to the "three refuges" and the five moral precepts.'

Questions

1) **Why did chanting develop and why did it remain a widespread practice even after the scriptures were committed to writing?**
2) **Why does Buddhism use chanting rather than hymn singing?**
3) **What is the meaning of the chant 'Namo Tassa Bhagavato, Arahato, Samasambuddhassa'?**

Further information for tasks set in students' book

Explain some of the ways in which Buddhists worship.

Key features of this answer might include:
- Reference to some of the reading mentioned above;
- An explanation of the importance of bowing in Buddhist countries. Respect for people and their attainments is thus directed at the memory of the Buddha;
- A description of the features of puja, e.g. offering of flowers, incense, water, etc. symbolising the five senses, and water for washing and drinking;
- An awareness of different practices in different schools of Buddhism, such as the use of mudra, mantra and mandala, prayer wheels and prayer flags;
- The use of chanting and music;
- The use of statues and pictures as objects of veneration, visualisation and meditation.

'The Buddha is not a god, so Buddhists do not worship him.' Evaluate the validity of this view.

Key features of this answer might include:
Arguments in favour of the proposition:
- The Buddha was just a man, and is now inaccessible to human beings;
- Some writers, for example Peter Harvey (Buddhism,.p125) argue that 'showing devotion to' is a better way of describing religious activities directed at the Buddha, and that the word 'worship is inappropriate, especially in a Theravada context.

Arguments against the proposition:
- It rather depends on what is meant by 'worship'. Certainly the Buddha is not a god (in fact he is considered to be more worthy than the gods), but it is through his attainment and teaching that others are able to find enlightenment. Thus he is worthy of worship;
- Mahayana Buddhists are more comfortable with the idea of worship, as they do not focus so much on the humanity of the Buddha. For them Buddhahood is the same as enlightenment itself, something beyond our understanding and cosmic in nature. Worshipping it is natural.

Extension task

Is Buddhism a religion?

Make a list of features that you think a religion should have. You might want to consider whether religions should have, for example, belief in an invisible world, belief in life after death, belief in God, belief in a correct way to live, an account of where suffering comes from. You might not want to include all, or even any, of these in your list.

Measure Buddhism against the criteria you have decided upon. Is Buddhism a religion?

Opportunities for Synoptic Element preparation

It would be advisable for students to make notes in preparation for the A2 Synoptic Assessment in areas which include:

- **Religious Authority**

  An awareness of the status of the Buddha, as a human teacher worthy of devotion, or a being of enlightenment worthy of worship?

- **Religious Experience**

  Experience of chanting and puja. The way in which controlling one's environment (use of incense, flowers, chanting etc.) can change one's mood, experience and state of mind.

- **Life, Death and Life After Death**

  Impermanence of life, as articulated by the use of impermanent sand or chalk mandalas.

From these elements of Indian culture Buddhism grew. The Buddha accepted, adapted or rejected certain elements of Indian society and belief.

The Buddha rejected

Caste ➡️ Because

Sacrifice ➡️ Because

Atman ➡️ Because

Concept of God ➡️ Because

The Buddha adapted the following to suit his purpose:

Reincarnation becomes rebirth ➡️ This means

Moksha becomes Enlightenment ➡️ This means

The Buddha accepted

Samsara ➡️

> He taught

Karma ➡️

> He taught

Meditation ➡️

> He taught

Self-discipline ➡️

> He taught

Buddhism for AS students : self-assessment form

Name:

Summarise the five main points you have learned though your study of this chapter:

-
-
-
-
-

Note the title of any written task that you have done during your study of this chapter: | *

-
-
-

*In this column, next to each task, give yourself a mark out of 5 that reflects how hard you worked on each of the tasks you did. 5 means 'very hard indeed', and 1 means 'not very hard at all.'

*Give yourself a mark out of 5 that reflects how well you think you understood the subject matter in this chapter. 5 means 'very well indeed', 1 means 'not much at all'. | *

List any topics to which you will have to give further attention before you understand them:

-
-
-

Note the chapter and details of any other book or website that you used whilst studying this chapter:

-
-
-
-

-
-
-
-

Note any particularly helpful quotations you came across which are relevant to your study of this chapter:

Author   Quotation

Answers to short questions for revision

1. **What is the Sanskrit word for soul?**

   atman

2. **What does tat tvam asi mean?**

   'That thou art' – that Brahman and atman are one.

3. **What does the phrase 'atman is Brahman' mean?**

   God and the Soul are the same – there is no differentiation between them.

4. **What is transmigration?**

   The movement of the soul from one life to the next.

5. **What is karma?**

   In Hinduism, the force which propels reincarnation. In Buddhism, the relationship between actions/intentions and consequences.

6. **What is moksha?**

   Liberation in Hinduism. Freeing the soul, or the uniting of the soul with god.

7. **What is dharma?**

   In Hinduism, dharma is religious duty. In Buddhism dharma is 'truth' or 'teaching'.

8. **Explain the varna system.**

   The traditional stratification of Hindu society based on levels of ritual purity. Birth into a particular varna was seen as the fruition of karma.

9. **Explain ritual purity.**

   The belief that some people are more pure than others, and the belief that a person's purity can, temporarily, be spoiled by contact with those less pure than themselves. Ritual purity is not about physical cleanliness, but about a 'ritual' state (i.e. it can be altered by actions and rituals).

10. **Why did sramanas break their ties with family and community?**

    Probably to enable them to concentrate on their spiritual goals, and in the belief that the attachments and responsibilities of family and community life would not be conducive to overcoming the needs and desires of the body.

11. **What does Shakyamuni mean?**

    Sage of the Shakya clan or tribe.

12. **Name the Buddha's parents.**

    Suddhodana and Yasodhara.

13. **What did Asita prophecy?**

    That if Siddhartha were prevented from seeing suffering, he would become a great leader of his people, but if he were to see suffering he would become a great religious teacher.

14. **What were the Four Sights?**

    Sickness, old age, death and the ascetic.

15. **Why did Siddhartha leave the palace?**

    Perhaps because he felt that his new knowledge about suffering and impermanence 'tainted' his life in the palace. He could no longer take pleasure in his life there because he knew that its vibrancy and beauty was temporary only.

16. **What did Siddhartha see during the first watch of the night under the Bodhi tree?**

    He saw his own former lives.

17. **Why is Nirvana difficult to define?**

Perhaps because it is a state that can't be described in words, because it is beyond everything we know. We have nothing to compare it to.

18. **What is Mahaparinirvana?**

The Great and Final Nirvana – the Buddha's death.

19. **Explain the Buddha's last words.**

'All conditioned things are perishable.' Everything in the world is impermanent. 'Work out your own salvation with diligence – be a lamp unto yourselves.' Follow your own path and work hard. Use yourself (and perhaps each other – the Sangha) as your guide.

20. **Explain why the Buddha's death is an inspiration to Buddhists.**

Perhaps because he let go of life peacefully, and had no attachments to cause him suffering. In a sense he had overcome death.

21. **What is the Sangha?**

The community of Buddhists. Sometimes the term refers strictly to the community of monks and nuns. The Sangha is the third of the three jewels.

22. **What is a stupa?**

Originally they were funeral mounds to enshrine the relics of kings. The Buddha's remains were enshrined in stupas, which went on to become the focus of devotion across the Buddhist world.

23. **What does Theravada mean?**

The Way of the Elders

24. **Why do Buddhists make offerings to statues?**

As a way of showing respect and veneration, and gratitude for what the Buddha has achieved in showing the way for others to attain enlightenment.

25. **Name a Mahayana Philosopher.**

Nagarjuna.

26. **What is Buddha-nature?**

The fundamentally enlightened nature of all beings.

27. **What does bodhisattva mean?**

Literally, 'enlightenment being.'

28. **What are Avalokitesvara's characteristics?**

Compassion. Sometimes he is presented as having thousands of arms to represent his ability to act compassionately, or many heads to show his superhuman knowledge of the sufferings of all beings.

29. **Name the Dhyani Buddhas.**

Aksobhya, Amoghasiddhi, Amitabha, Vairocana and Ratnasambhava.

30. **Explain Lin Chi's instruction 'if you see the Buddha in your path, kill him'.**

You should be free of attachments even to teachers such as the Buddha.

31. **What is the relationship between Wisdom and Compassion?**

Because truth is the connected nature of all things, someone who acts wisely will naturally act compassionately.

32. **What is dukkha?**

Sometimes translated as suffering, the term dukkha has many meanings. As well as suffering it also means 'unsatisfactoriness' and 'frustration'. It is the first of the four noble truths and the one of the laksanas, or marks of existence.

33. **What is anicca?**

Impermanence. One of the laksanas or marks of existence.

34. **What is anatta?**

No-fixed self. The view that there is nothing about the person which persists eternally, without change. One of the laksanas or marks of existence.

35. **What are pretas?**

Hungry Ghosts. One of the realms of existence as depicted in the wheel of life.

36. **What does the parable of the poisoned arrow illustrate?**

That the human condition is not helped by metaphysical speculation. The situation of suffering in which we find ourselves requires urgent attention, and asking questions about things that, even if we could get actual answers to them (which is in doubt) will not help us to address our situation, is misguided.

37. **Why can the Buddha not be described as an eternalist?**

Because he taught that everything was impermanent.

38. **What central Buddhist doctrine does Nagasena illustrate with his metaphor of the chariot?**

Anatta – no fixed- self.

49. **What is the Middle Way?**

The Buddhist way which avoids extreme lifestyles (of either pleasure or asceticism) and extreme views (such as nihilism or eternalism).

40. **What is karma?**

The relationship between intentions/actions and consequences. Karma is an inexorable force in Buddhism, but it can be purified.

41. **What is anatta?**

No-self. The view that there is nothing about the person that persists eternally, without change.

43. **What is the Bhavacakra?**

The Wheel of life, which depicts the way in which ignorance leads to sickness, old age and death, the way in which samsara is driven by the three fires or poisons of greed, hatred and delusion (ignorance). It also shows the six realms of existence, and the power of karma.

44. **What is Pratitya Samutpada?**

Interdependent Origination. The truth that all things are fundamentally linked and connected to each other.

44. **What is the difference between rebirth and reincarnation?**

Reincarnation is the soul entering a body anew. Rebirth is the fruition of karma from a past life. In other words it is the idea that one life was caused by a previous life, but that there is not a straightforward continuity between the two lives.

45. **What are the six realms?**

The realms into which it is possible to reborn, as depicted in the wheel of life. Sometimes these are understood as psychological states rather than as actually existing realms.

46. **How is ignorance symbolised in the first of the twelve links?**

By a blind man.

47. **Explain the symbolism of the hungry ghost.**

The hungry ghosts symbolises insatiable craving. With large stomachs and thin necks they can never satisfy their hunger, and the streams from which they attempt to drink are ablaze.

48. **Explain why the three fires/poisons are depicted at the hub of the wheel.**

Perhaps because they drive the wheel of becoming. They keep unenlightened beings locked in the endless round of samsara.

49. **What is panna?**

Wisdom. One of the aspects of the Eightfold Path.

50. **What is sila?**

Morality. One of the aspects of the Eightfold Path.

51. **What is samadhi?**

Meditation. One of the aspects of the Eightfold Path.

52. **What is dana?**

'Giving'. Lay people offer dana to the Sangha and in doing so gain merit.

53. **What are the paramitas?**

The 'Perfections': giving, morality, energy, patience, meditation, wisdom.

54. **How does the Eightfold Path help Buddhists to tread the 'Middle Way'?**

By directing attention to all aspects of life, so that a more wholesome life can be cultivated.

55. **What are the three jewels?**

Buddha, Dharma and Sangha.

56. **What is the Sangha?**

The community of Buddhists, in the wide sense. Strictly, the community of monks and nuns.

57. **What is going for refuge?**

The ritual of formally turning to the Buddha, the Dharma and the Sangha, the supports of the Buddhist life.

58. **What are the precepts?**

These are goals towards which the Buddhist orientates herself. There are five lay precepts, and ten monastic ones. There are also 227 patimokka rules that regulate the conduct of the monastic Sangha.

59. **What is merit?**

Puñña, or merit, is the good karma which results from actions which are positive. Merit is usually offered to others, i.e. one does not do good things for the sake of one's own progress, one does it for others, often for deceased relatives.

60. **What are the monastic precepts?**

There are 10 monastic precepts, which include the five lay precepts, plus abstaining from eating after midday, from dancing or singing, from using perfume or adornments, from sleeping on a comfortable bed, or from handling money.

61. **What is the Vinaya Pitaka?**

The portion of the Pali Canon which contains the code of conduct for monks and nuns.

62. **Explain the importance of the 'Three Jewels' in Buddhism'?**

The three jewels (triratna) of Buddha, Dharma and Sangha are tightly linked with each other. They form three key aspects of the Buddhism, and feature on Buddhist iconography. Buddhists go for refuge in the three jewels, which demonstrates their orientation towards a Buddhist lifestyle and away from a materialistic one.

63. **What is Samatha?**

Calmness meditation.

64. **What is Vipassana?**

Insight meditation.

65. **What is Zazen?**

Sitting meditation.

66. **What is metta bhavana?**

Loving-kindness meditation.

67. **What are the Brahmaviharas?**

The four godlike states loving-kindness, compassion, sympathetic joy and equanimity.

68. **Explain the Pure Land Buddhist attitude to meditation.**

Pure Land Buddhists believe that human beings are too corrupt and karma bound to be able to make any spiritual progress of their own. Therefore, they do not meditate, but rely on the power of Amida to being them to enlightenment.

69. **What is a mudra?**

A hand gesture which symbolises an aspect of enlightenment.

70. **What is a mantra?**

A phrase containing the name of an enlightened being which is repeated in order to manifest the qualities of that enlightened being.

71. **What is a mandala?**

A mandala is a diagram of the cosmos that also depicts the spiritual path. It is circular and often shows a number of enlightened beings. The mandala is used in visualisation and meditation. Sometimes mandalas are made using coloured powders and chalks.

72. **What is puja?**

Worship. Ritual veneration of the image of the Buddha or other enlightened beings.

73. **Why do some Buddhists chant the mantra Om mani padme hum?**

It is the mantra of Avalokitesvara Bodhisattva, and when it is chanted Avalokitesvara's compassion is manifested.

74. **Why are mandalas sometimes washed away?**

As a reminder of impermanence.

Part Two: Specimen answers

Question

The time when he really began to think about life occurred at the age of 29. According to the commentaries and legends, the young 'prince' had led a very sheltered life, with all possible luxuries, deliberately kept away from all experience of sickness, old age or death in an attempt by his father to prevent him renouncing the world as the prophecies had foretold. However, on excursions from the palaces with his charioteer Channa, he saw four sights that changed his life. These were a tired, wrinkled, worn out old man, a man in great pain with a diseased body, a corpse being taken to the cremation ground, and a religious ascetic.

Buddhism, Denise Cush

(a) Explain why his father had tried to make sure that the Buddha did not see sickness, old age and death. [10]
(b) Explain the effect on the Buddha of seeing the old man, the sick man, and the corpse. [10]

Mark scheme

(a) Because of the belief that if the harsher side of life is not experienced one has no cause to question its meaning, or the cause of suffering, or to seek the way of liberation. He was trying to avoid the fulfilment of one of the birth prophecies, and to ensure that Siddhartha remained loyal to his caste duty as a Kshatriya. 10 AO1

(b) He realised that all beings, including his family and himself, are subject to sickness, old age and death. This new knowledge touched and tainted everything, and led to his rejection of his life in the palace. It brought on a 'dark night of the soul' type of despair. 10 AO1

Script A

(a) When Siddhartha was born his father was told in a prophecy by Asita that he would either become a great king or a holy man if he was to see the 4 signs, so his father guarded his son from being able to see these signs as his father wanted Siddhartha to become a great king just as he was. As Cush says, the reason he did this was to prevent him renouncing the world as one of the prophecies had foretold. If he did this it would mean he would not be a king like his father, but a holy man and his father didn't want that.

Examiner's comments

This answer does not go very far. It accurately identifies the prophecy as the source of the decision. However, there is no evidence that the candidate understands why the Four Signs might have an undesirable effect on Siddhartha, or why Suddhodana would have wanted him to become a King other than to be like him. The candidate does refer to the stimulus in the answer, but does no more than quote from it. The lack of scope in this answer keeps it to a level 2, 4 marks.

(b) After seeing the four signs on outings from the palace Siddhartha realised how shallow and empty his life actually was within the walls of the palace, and just how little he actually knew about life itself. These four sights changed Siddhartha's life forever. They inspired Siddhartha to leave the luxury of his palace life and go out into the world to find and answer to the questions he had.

Examiner's comments

The answer is accurate but minimal. There is no sense of the pain that Siddhartha experienced on realising the transitoriness of life. The candidate describes his sense of ignorance, and his realisation that his life was 'shallow and empty' (an excellent phrase), but he or she doesn't explain why he felt that way. There is no sense in this answer of Siddhartha having been brought suddenly face to face with the human condition, and the shock and despair that he felt at such a realisation late in life, and the effect that sickness old age and death would not have not only on himself, but those that he loved. Level 2, 4 marks.

Script B

(a) The Buddha's father did not want the Buddha to see sickness, old age or death because they would make Siddhartha think about holy questions. The whole reason for Siddhartha's father keeping him in a sheltered life in the palace was to stop him from thinking about the ultimate questions which may make him renounce the world. Sights like these prompt holy questions like what happens after death and make siddhartha realise that it would happen to him and his family too. Siddhartha's father was especially concerned because he wanted him to grow up to be a ruler like himself but the prophecies made at Siddhartha's birth worried him.

Examiner's comments

This candidate has focused on the crucial issue – that seeing the four sights would lead Siddhartha to ask serious, religious questions about the meaning of life and suffering - and explains this very well. The candidate does not refer to the fact that it would be Siddhartha's religious duty to follow in his father's footsteps, but the candidates has done sufficient here to get a good level 4, 8 marks.

(b) What the Buddha saw the first three of the passing sights – the old man, sick man or the corpse, it made Siddhartha feel very sad and probably shocked too. Because the Buddha had led such a sheltered life, he had never seen any sign of these three things before. Siddhartha was upset because he realised it was going to happen to him and the people he loved and he couldn't stop it. For the first time, Siddhartha realised impermanence. The Buddha was also angry at first with his father for not allowing him to know the truth about life.

Examiner's comments

The candidate demonstrates facility with technical terms, and an insight into the feelings that Siddhartha may have felt, both for himself and for others. The candidates demonstrates awareness of the fundamental nature of his realisation when he/she states, 'for the first time, Siddhartha realised impermanence.' This shows insight worthy of a level 4, 8 marks.

Question

(a) Explain the Four Noble Truths. [10]

(b) Assess the view that it is difficult to accept that 'All life is dukkha'. [10]

Mark scheme

(a) Answers will recast the Four Noble Truths (all life is dukkha, dukkha is caused by attachment, attachment and therefore dukkha, can be overcome, the way to overcome attachment, and therefore dukkha is to follow the eightfold path) in candidates own words, and will draw on illustrations and examples for explanatory purposes. 10 AO1

(b) If dukkha meant simply 'suffering' then it would be impossible to accept the first noble truth. Some people, especially those of a monotheistic persuasion, would find the Buddha's description of reality as difficult to accept because it denies the perfection of creation (in fact it makes no reference to creation at all). Candidates may offer examples to illustrate why the notion of dukkha is an appealing and explanatory one. 10 AO2

Script A

(a) After living in luxuries and then practising austerities, the Buddha then realised the Four Noble Truths.
1. All life is Dukkha
2. Because of dukkha there is tanha
3. To eliminate dukkha we must eliminate tanha
4. Follow the eightfold path

The Buddha saw all life as unsatisfactory. Even something nice eg. Holiday is dukkha because it has to end sometime. Everything changes all the time (anicca) except for nirvana and space. As all life is dukkha, there is a craving (tanha) for different things in life, and to get rid of dukkha we need to stop craving.

To reach nirvana you must follow the eightfold path for which you must have the
Right mindfulness
Right livelihood
Right speech
Right action
Right thought
Right concentration

Examiner's comments
The candidate does not know the second noble truth (the cause of dukkha is tanha). However, apart from that, and two missing factors of the eightfold path, a fair amount of knowledge is shown. there is one attempt at 'explanation' (the trigger word in the question was 'explain') but not sufficient for the candidate to be described as having 'reasonable' rather than 'limited' understanding. Level 2, 3 marks.

(b) It is difficult to accept that 'all life is dukkha' because when you are happy, life doesn't seem unsatisfactory.

Examiner's comments
This answer barely gets off the ground. Level 1, 1 mark.

Script B

(a) The four noble truths are the basic teachings of Buddhism. Once they are understood and realised, you are no longer ignorant to the ways of the world, you realise it and can escape from samsara.

The four noble Truths are:
1 all life is dukkha,
2, the cause of dukkha is tanha (craving)
3, the way to eliminate dukkha is to eliminate tanha,
4, to do this, follow the eightfold path.

The first of the truths is 'all life is dukkha . The word dukkha does not translate very well into English scholars eg Merv Fowler in his book Buddhism – beliefs and practices says that the best translation is unsatisfactoriness. Some eg Denise Cush – Buddhism say that it is translated as suffering but this tends to bring about the idea of suffering being sickness, disease, etc. which is suffering but does not cover the whole 'spectrum' of dukkha.

There are three types of Dukkha. The first being watching people suffer through illness disease especially if these people are loved ones. The second type is the desire for things that we can't have. Nowadays advertisements cause the craving of material things. These objects are more than likely not needed and you are probably unable to afford them, but still you crave them. Knowing that you cannot have the objects causes un-happiness, which causes dukkha.

The third type is for example a favourite toy gets broken or worn out. You become upset by this as your realise that it does not last for ever. This is the concept of anicca, impermanence. Nothing is permanent, everything is in a constant state of flux. Nothing will last. Eg having a perfect holiday – at the time it seems perfect and completely satisfactory but then it ends, which leads to unhappiness.

The second truth is 'the cause of dukkha is tanha.' As said previously, everybody wants things that they cannot have. This causes unhappiness. If we didn't crave things then we wouldn't be disappointed that we cannot have the items.
The third truth – 'the way to eliminate dukkha is to eliminate tanha.' If you understand the concept of anicca, nothing being permanent, then you realise that it is pointless craving things as they will end - which will cause unhappiness leading to dukkha. It is cyclic unless you realise it, you cannot eliminate it. They fuel each other. If we do not crave things then you will not become disappointed by the fact that you cannot get them due to many reasons eg lack of money.

The fourth truth is 'follow the eightfold path.' The Eightfold Path consists of
Right understanding – of the senses
Right thought
Right speech – no gossiping/swearing & others
Right action
Right livelihood – having a job that doesn't harm others
Right effort
Right mindfulness
Right concentration

If you follow all these steps it will lead to enlightenment. This would make you a Buddha and you could escape from samsara and enter nirvana. All the truths are interrelated. If you have tanha, it cause dukkha, and the only way to eliminate this is to follow the eightfold path. The eightfold path also helps with issues in life eg the 3,4,5, parts are concerned with morality and ethics, 6, 7, 8 help with meditation – the Buddhist practice whilst 1 & 2 are wisdom.

All these aspects help Buddhists be guided. They turn to the path when they need help as it the basis by how the Buddha found enlightenment and therefore is extremely important to Buddhists.

Examiner's comments

This answer is thorough, detailed and accurate. The candidate refers helpfully to scholars, which whilst not essential at AS level is one way of providing the 'evidence and examples' required at level five. The candidate demonstrates understanding by using his/her own examples, such as reference to worn-out toys, advertising, holidays etc. the candidates demonstrates a very sophisticated understanding of the nature of craving, and how realising the truth of anicca is an antidote to it. The candidate also highlights the centrality of the fourth truth in Buddhist practice and the Buddha's own life. Level 5, 10 marks.

(b) If you are not a Buddhist then it is very difficult to accept that view. Non-Buddhists probably recognise the fact that anything is going to come to an end, so when for example, taking the perfect holiday, they enjoy it while it lasts as they realise that it will actually end. They prepare themselves for disappointment in a way. Non-Buddhists would probably find this view difficult to accept as they find their lives satisfactory, eg having family house car etc. and could not possibly think that because there is no soul, or nothing is permanent, that it would make their life unsatisfactory.

However Buddhists at first probably found it hard to accept this view as they realised all possessions are impermanent as is the belief in anatta, there being no soul. However, as they become used to the Buddhist truths they are no longer living in ignorance of the truth. They can strive on and attempt to reach nirvana and free themselves from samsara. They realise the truth and by doing this can eliminate dukkha.

Examiner's comments

Different points of view are considered here though there is a lack of clarity in the answer, and no firm evidence that the candidate realises that some may see the Buddhist understanding of dukkha as tainting everything as rather negative, though it is possible that the candidate means to convey this at the end of his/her first paragraph. There is no awareness that people may reject the idea that there is no happiness in this life for religious reasons. Level 3, 5 marks.

Advice about trips

When visiting Buddhist centres, communities or temples in Britain, all the usual advice applies, in relation to planning; building a project around your visit; getting parental permission; clarifying your needs for the people you are visiting; preparing the students in advance for questions; giving instructions on orderly and quiet behaviour; and formally thanking your hosts, both at the end of the visit and by letter afterwards. Buddhist communities vary a great deal, and it is essential to ascertain the type of Buddhism that is practised at your chosen destination, both so that students are properly prepared and so that matters of etiquette are not breached.

Unlike visits to mosques or gurdwaras, there are not normally any issues regarding clothing, though modest dress is advisable, especially when visiting a monastic Sangha. Students should be prepared to remove their shoes when instructed to.

It is worth clarifying in advance how to make a donation. Theravada Bhikkhus (monks) and Siladharis (nuns), as well as monks and nuns in some other traditions, are not allowed to handle money, but it is usually possible to make a donation at a monastery office, or by post. Members of the monastic Sangha are not allowed to touch members of the opposite sex, so it's best to avoid handshaking in these cases.

It is a good idea to clarify for your hosts, in advance, the level of understanding that your students have reached. Sometimes it is helpful to mention some of the books they have read. It is also helpful to give your hosts an idea of the kinds of questions your students are likely to ask.

Establish in advance whether photographs are permitted. Students should be prevented from snapping indiscriminately.

Students should be encouraged to ask questions about a range of issues, not only about lifestyle or the classic teachings of Buddhism. It is interesting to discover the positions of different Buddhists on a range of ethical issues — on the aims and objectives of the activities which go on at that particular centre, the ethnic background of members, attitudes towards other religions, their views on politics, sexuality, education, a particular issue currently in the news and so on.

At some centres it might be possible to invite your hosts to lead a simple meditation for your students. Make sure that your students are prepared for this, and are free not to participate if they have religious objections to doing so. Depending on who is in your class, you may need to seek permission in advance from your hosts for a student to leave the room at this point, although usually students who don't wish to participate are happy to watch, and gain a great deal from doing so. There are very few religious beliefs that are compromised by a simple breathing meditation, so such a situation rarely arises. However, it is important that the autonomy of pupils is respected.

Having the opportunity to experience meditation in this way is a real privilege, and since Buddhism is an experiential religion (Buddhists often say that until you've actually experienced it, you cannot understand it) having such an opportunity might be regarded as almost essential to a study of Buddhism.

The Buddhist Society produces an annual Buddhist Directory, which gives the contact details of a great many of the Buddhist groups and centres in Britain. Some centres have websites, which students can peruse before the trip. The Buddhist Directory gives details of these.

The directory can be purchased from:
The Buddhist Society
58 Eccleston Square
London
SW1V 1PH

Tel 020 7834 5858
Fax 020 7976 5238
http://www.thebuddhistsociety.org.uk

Some of the smaller Buddhist groups are simply like-minded people who get together in someone's home for meditation. Visits to these groups are not usually worthwhile, as there is often nothing much to see. However, a visit to school by a member of one of these groups can be extremely worthwhile

Bibliography

Armstrong, Karen, *Buddha*, London, Orion, 2002

Carrithers, Michael, *The Buddha*, Oxford, Oxford University Press, 1990

Clarke, Steve & Thompson, Mel, *Buddhism: A New Approach*, London, Hodder & Stoughton, 1996 (designed for KS4 but useful for AS)

Conze Edward, *Buddhist Scriptures*, Harmondsworth, Penguin, 1959

Cush, Denise, *Buddhism*, London, Hodder & Stoughton, 1993

Erricker, Clive, *Teach Yourself Buddhism*, London, Hodder & Stoughton, 2003

Fowler, Merv, *Buddhism, Beliefs and Practices*, Brighton, Sussex Academic Press, 1999

Gethin, Rupert, *The Foundations of Buddhism*, Oxford, Oxford University Press, 1998

Gombrich, Richard, *Theravada Buddhism: a social history from ancient Benares to modern Colombo*, London, Routledge, 1988

Harris, Elizabeth, *What Buddhists Believe,* Oxford, Oneworld, 1998

Harvey, Peter, *An Introduction to Buddhism: Teachings, History and Practices*, Cambridge, Cambridge University Press, 1990

Harvey, Peter (ed), *Buddhism*, London, Continuum, 2001

Keown, Damien, *Buddhism: A Very Short Introduction*, Oxford, Oxford University Press, 1996

Skilton, Andrew, *A Concise History of Buddhism*, Birmingham, Windhorse, 1997

Snelling, John, *The Buddhist Handbook: A complete guide to Buddhist teaching and practice*, London, Rider, 1987

Thompson, Mel, *101 Key Ideas: Buddhism*, London, Hodder & Stoughton, 2000

Williams, Paul, *Mahayana Buddhism: The Doctrinal Foundations*, London, Routledge, 1989